LIFE ON THE ROCKS

SOME THOUGHTS IN INK WHILE YOU ENJOY YOUR DRINK

THE BARTENDING POET

Dear "Deer"

Your watch is the billboard

The time is my ad

When you see 12:34 on the face,

Remember to smile; Remember me

Contents

Contents

Contents

Prologue

I found the world was hard to understand
I searched for meaning in words written by dead
While I stood behind the bar, serving people at day's end
I often talked to souls with defeated head

I saw their hopes and dreams that always got dashed
I felt their anguish and pain, and yearning desire to get heard
I listened to their words which were left unsaid
And I decided to leave the trail of their stories, simply penned

SIGNING OFF FROM LOVE

A Poet's Prescription for a Delusion called Love

In pursuit of 'true' love, people often disregard the person around them; their anchor and the one carrying them forward.

And some can also forget the sacrifices made by their partners, and aimlessly look for their 'perfect' soulmate.

All of this can lead to suffering and a melancholic environment, which hurts the very people who 'deserve' the so called 'true' love.

This chapter is dedicated to those who are hidden in our hearts but in plain sight, and loving us unconditionally.

'Sign-off' from the delusion of love, and just see what is there...

2

Ink Fall

I wish to tell, the tale of "love in fall"
In words to paint this mural, on time's wall
A palette of past with no colours that are dull
Strokes on paper, that swim, fly and crawl

Letters are notes of the music called prose
Pen is the conductor, it's hard to get those
The ink has run out, song is still long
This orchestra is shut, no point to play broke

3 Permission

I want to know, your story, your journey
I want to know, what you've seen
I want to know, places you've gone
I want to know, your mystery and travesty

I am asking for your permission

All this time, I've grown restless
I can't stop thinking, it's just senseless
Past won't change and I'll open the wounds
But I am obsessed to know you, out of bounds

4 Hold On

You know your strength
Just let me explain
You know you aren't alone
I can see the pain

♡♡♡

You know you can get through
Nothing is in vain
You know you will find the shade
It's just the rain

5

The Return

My silence is not true
It's pain that's unsaid
I hope you can see
I know you understand

♡♡♡

Everything that aches
Is a reminder of hell
Past that's gone
I remained tense and unwell

♡♡♡

Just give me a moment
To recover back to health
I may take some time
To come back to you with a smile

6

Rise in Love

I wish to tell, the tale of "love in fall"
In words to paint this mural, on time's wall
A palette of past with no colours that are dull
Strokes on paper, that swim, fly and crawl

Letters are notes of the music called prose
Pen is the conductor, it's hard to get those
The ink has run out, song is still long
This orchestra is shut, no point to play broke

7

Girl Inside

Gazing outside, looking for meaning
It's inside, she needs to keep searching
Eyes betray what she is bewildered about
She knows the thousand lies and the real truth

Face is deceiving the ones who look
She knows the world by the book
Those lips pursed, ready to demolish you
But relax first, you won't find an issue

8

Only, Maybe, Sometimes

If only, may be, sometimes
We will kiss under the stars
If only, may be, sometimes
We will sleep in each other's arms

If only, may be, sometimes
I will find that love divine
If only, may be, sometimes
Your flower will blossom on your grave site

9

Death By Chocolate

I offered a rose, a red regret
Ended up in making her upset
"Let’s be friend", she tried to explain
These words were seared forever in my brain

I can’t figure out what her intentions
I didn’t know what she expected
This aching heart is looking for conclusion
Death by Chocolate, seems perfect end

10

Silent Star

I am not just a Silent Star
Let me be the Guiding one too
I know what the answers are
Let me tell the reasons true

♡♡♡

I see your trials and tribulations
I have gone through the same
I haven't just become bright overnight
I have burned and travelled for a million years

11

Satanic Tears

I prayed, then cried, on my knees
I couldn’t fathom, I'm still in disbelief
Wrath of a woman everyone fears
And I saw revenge in her satanic tears

But someone held me through these times
Helped me find myself and hang the chimes
My struggles have finally given me bliss
And bless my stars for her angelic kiss

12

Your Remedy

I was looking for name and validation
I was searching for fame and acceptance
From the world which questioned my existence
I never knew that there is no answer

You made me believe in myself again
You told me to see the goodness that I keep
You taught me love is what we all need
You are my beautiful dream, I just want to sleep

13

Redemption

You left a hole, in my heart that I behold
I will remember you in my prayers unheard
I will miss waiting for you words to be told
I will carve out your name on every stone unturned

Forever in memories, you will be etched
Like a kaleidoscope, they will project
My sins may have brought this unwanted end
I pray for my redemption and your journey to heaven

14

I Tried

I tried to save you, you wanted to drown
I crossed oceans, all you did was frown
It was my duty, my way to redemption
You took it away, for your addiction

I give it up, I won't care now
I cared enough, to make you safe somehow
I need to move on, and live my life
It may be too late, but I am still alive

15

Gone

Fading away is memory of yours
I don't remember the last time we kissed
Feelings have now turned sour
Down the hole, drains my love to the ground

I need a new heart to rest my soul
I belong to a better place to dwell
I suffered enough to get a pass out of hell
I will venture the promised land of love they tell

16

Longing

Chance to live by your side
Was something I always aspired
I lost it when I went after my desires
Time can't return if I turn back dials

I have to live with my choices
Knowing they have their price
Longing for getting second chance
I will wait for destiny to stop its dance

17

No Bliss

Girl inside you're broken
But too outspoken
And you always have an opinion
But never a humble one
And I don't find any bliss

♡♡♡

And I won't sing to make you pleased
So I start my own journey
To the end of this travesty
And find my own destiny
Else end up in anonymity
And I don't find any bliss

♡♡♡

And I won't laugh to make you smile
And I don't find any bliss
And I won't come to give you a kiss
So far far away, I leave you, today
And I will find my truth, someday
But I don't find any bliss

I'll be gone and you're gonna miss

18

Demons

Yes, for you, I sold my soul
Begged at pedestal of hell
Nothing's fine but I act well
You won't know, you're swell

Black tar heart of yours
Filled with contempt of years
Drowning me in wasted tears
You'll stop when my hide you wear

I don't have anything left to sacrifice
But nothing will ever suffice
You'll need my soul twice
Even demons won't feel nice

19

Meaning of Us

Hey, what you whispered and went away
I am lost and bewildered with your words
Wait and stay for me, I won't sway
This time I would be there with you and stay

And I surrender, my soul to you
I want you but want is not true
Staring in starry night till it turns blue
I will explain my love for you

Soon you will realize, I am for you
You corrode my ego into harsh truth
Finally you will feel my pulse
Lost in translation in meaning of us

20

Fresh Dew

There is nothing to see new
No words which are due
Morning scent and birds few
And you lie beside me on fresh dew

Let me capture this moment
I have lived in world of torment
This revives me and gives me semblance
As you lie beside me on fresh dew

Open your arms, hold me now
Take this hurt and pain away
Bring me close and turn me new
As you lie beside me on fresh dew

Talk to me, take me to the promised land
The place I always dreamt and wondered
Make me believe, in all my dreams

As you lie beside me on fresh dew

ᑭᑭᑭ

Now I wake up, I search for you
There is reminiscent of you makeup
And I feel ever close to you again
Like you lied beside me on fresh dew

21

My Apologies

Revenge cursed the soul of mine
So I sought to bring it down
Chokes it and let it drown
It was the moment, don't frown

♡♡♡

I know you wanted me to take it
But I have moved on, can't fake it
It's a fire that burns the conscience to ash
Better not to repent later and crash

22

Moves

Strangers in the bar, racing thoughts
Surprised at each other's drink bought
Both want to kiss and make out
Oceans of distance is there to put out

Make the move and grab her in your arms
Take her away and lie beside lake of calm
Stare at the sky, bestowed with starry night
Listen to her breath and never leave her side

Kiss her and let her feel your love
Take her to the place where she can be herself
Light a fire, and speak your heart out
There are no second chances for you to let it out

23

First Time

Trying to forget, looking for bliss
It's just not me, you also remember the kiss
It was raining, our first time at lab of Physics
You were blushing, nothing was amiss

I can't remember when I first cried
I just know that I haven't tried
You left me alone, I was full of pride
Now I will regret this, till I die

24

Waiting

On the sidewalk, I look for you
I know you've gone, but it's untrue
For every spark in eyes, I picture you
Death can't make us apart, feelings do

♡♡♡

I will wait for you till the eternity
Dying alone isn't in my destiny
Just search for a man lost in insanity
You will find my soul in these dark streets

25

Move On

Let's talk and resolve this
I don't hate you, I want peace
Lay down you terms, let me see
I will be reasonable, as much as I can be

♡♡♡

Settling differences is what I want
Why dig graves in each other's front
Each of us has to make our ego bent
Find a way to let the anger out and to vent

♡♡♡

Believe me one last time
Future will be going to be just fine
I will move away from your line
You have the chance to define

26

Whispers of Tomorrow

Words I lost
Sounds of her voice
Self-doubt I lost
Power of her Love

Cries of Past, Forget them
Shouts of Today, Ignore them
Silence your mind in the time that you borrow
You will hear finally, Whispers of Tomorrow

27

First Love

Mind played tricks, when it didn't understand
Her side stares, seem like an invitation unsaid
Heart skipped a beat, on her first words of behest
I waited for the coffee, and an awkward request

♡♡♡

I made a million dreams, on one single glance
I composed a song, for our wedding dance
It's hard to fathom, she is not serving coffee
My first love was she and she wanted her country free

♡♡♡

I stand here, at her wake
Few words were said, a body laid to rest
A guard of honour in her respect
An incomplete story, few tears of regret

28

Final Embrace

There are no words spoken
There are no promises made
There are no letters written
There are no treaties framed

We learned to live within space
Between words in every sentence
We understand in exchanged gaze
Between thoughts for a final embrace

29
PART TWO

SILENCE & SORROWS

Poetic expression of grief, tragedy, silence and sorrows

ღღღ

30

Pale Red Moon

Pale red moon, let him bleed
He danced in tears, his misdeed
His black soul, looking for creed
Lust for angels, his dire need

Pale red moon, take him afar
He worsened enough, his inside turned to tar
Moths are coming, to light of the car
His body lies, like an unstrung guitar

31 Addiction

I can't breathe, smoke is filled in
Each drag makes it shorter, life that is
It started with you, and will end with me
We shared the first one, last one will take me

I can't sleep, the faces are in deep
Each drink sketched one, erasing me
Cheers for us and down the drain for me
Drunk in an alleyway, now I am on my knees

32

Pulling the Trigger

She asked me for unconditional love
And a promise to be there forever
I missed my father's funeral
To aid in my own son's birth

A decade later, I am sitting here alone
A park with toddlers and elders no one wants
I realise I was used as a 'donor', can never be a father
I am lost but can't even think of pulling the trigger

33

In Your Eyes

In your eyes, I see the cliff
Where thousands dreams have committed suicide
In your eyes, I see the souls
Trapped in the abyss, can't lose the confines

In your eyes, I see dark deals
Ways to trick devil to build a God's shrine
In your eyes, I see the vacuum
That even suffocated your heart dry

34
Clouds that Cry

I rode the waves, when I gave my will a try,
I confronted storms, when I wanted to feel alive,
I went against the ocean breeze, when I wanted to fly my kite,
I was never alone and found company,
When my dad died, wept with clouds that cry

35

Lanes of Memories

A glance of her eyes has caught my attention
I served a free drink, to know her intentions
A conversation began, wasn't just a discussion
Transversed through time, lost space in our perceptions

Five years past, I saw her sitting on a station
People went passed, no one had compassion
An intelligent mind, under confusion and delusion
Running in "lanes of memories", lost in translation

36

Lost Man

Bringing in, the waves tell a story
Lonely island a host to misery
Drenched in rain, he walks towards a brewery
To drown his sorrows and hoping for recovery

Desperate times made him a criminal
It wasn't his choice, it was destiny's betrayal
Lives he ruined are not just his fault
He was damned right from the start

37

Vanishing in the Ether Unseen

Drizzling down the sky, those tears don't mean a lot
Whatever I have found, lost purpose and bears a cost
Maybe someday, I will see find my own muse to plot
Finally I can reach the bottom of this huge pit

I couldn't outrun my mind, it's in split
I have realized what it actually meant
I finally found a way to climb out
Prom this abyss, filled with broken dreams and guilt

I have to confess something, before I leave
My words are all up choked inside
Clinging on my throat and I struggle to reveal
Listen to me, before I begin to fade

Remember the words, as I vanish in the ether unseen.

38

Prayer

Chiselled by your repression
Soul is full of apprehension
Pain is my new dimension
This is your only contribution

Out of the saddle, horses run
Riding devil, waiting for turn
Fire of hell is ready to burn
My ashes will turn up in your urn

Take care, flow them away
Do it before it turns to day
Consider this, try your sway
Demons may leave me to stay

39

My Days

Do you remember my days
When I was free to say
Gazing stars in green fields
Insanity wasn't my shield

Do you remember the time
When my paintings were sublime
Staring out the window aimlessly
Madness wasn't creeping silently

40 Alive

In ICU, motionlessly lying
Contemplating there's nothing in dying
World moves on like river flowing
It's better to go out raising flag high and flying

It's a new birth, but no labour pain
Only mother is world's disdain
Nothing is left to waste in vain
New beginning and goals to attain

Now, I breathe in the blue sky
Appreciate my kid's smile
Get lost in beauty and admire
I am no longer dead inside, but alive

41

Damned Soldier

Light the candles around the grave
Pray for the one who died brave
He fought for children to make them safe
But killed the child soldiers, his mistake

He was damned and trapped
He needed to find an escape
Moral reasons kept him at bay
But bullets don't have ethics and shame

42

We are all Jokers in this Life

Justice delayed is justice denied
Officers of court seem like they never cried
Knowing the pain, always looking for a dime
Enabling corruption, letting go crime
Resting my case, give me next prompt line

We are all Jokers in this life
One-man show to please Kids and wife
Entertaining their wishes and whines
Looking for Reasons for whiskey and wine

43

Silence of You

I wanted them to hear my voice
They had to bear, didn't have a choice
But all I heard back, was echo in a void
No one LISTENED, to a word that I said

Slowly I realised, I need to express myself better
I learnt the language of Silence, my words are now louder than ever
Now I realise who I am and the world doesn't matter
Even your shadow leaves you in the darkness, so why care?

It's not grief that brings me down
It's not betrayal that makes me frown
It's not in sorrow that I get drowned
It's not a regret that I have found

It's an unfathomable anger to hold
Its an unspeakable crime to process
It was a kid's body that brought a flash flood
Of tears, a dam broken by people's indifference

45

No Wait to Stay

Divine is what it feels like today
Scattered dreams brush away
Make another castle they say
Have a drink and dance today

In my time, I have been blessed
They have given, what I deserved
Hope and Destiny, names they possess
I don't mind, what they profess

Tomorrow will be my last day at this place
They have told me to give it a rest
What I waited for, has already been dressed
In the attire of magnanimity, with a crest

46

Crying with Angels

I laughed with my friends
I smiled with my love
I battled with my men
I danced with my wife

I am not the man you think
I had my own miseries
I did make a deal with the devil
Crying with angels, my only bliss

47

Quicksand

I don't know how to make castles
Petrified, by all of the world's hassles
I find it difficult to lay the foundation
Of a new life, away from complication

I don't know why, why you pull me back
Tired, by all your emotional blackmail
Trying to get out of this abyss
I might succeed with a chance to miss

48

Destiny's Betrayal

Bringing in, the waves tell a story
Lonely island a host to misery
Drenched in rain, he walks towards a brewery
To drown his sorrows and hoping for recovery

Desperate times made him a criminal
It wasn't his choice, it was destiny's betrayal
Lives he ruined are not just his fault
He was damned right from the start

49

Memory

Do you remember my days
When I was free to say
Gazing stars in green fields
Insanity was my only shield

Do you remember the time
When my paintings were sublime
Staring out the window aimlessly
Madness wasn't creeping silently

Do you remember my son
When he cried for what he had done
Sleeping in crouching position
Leaving me in teary situation

Do you remember his death
When he took his last breath
This juxtaposition doesn't make sense

Like my life which hasn't been so dense

SMILE FOR SANITY

A compilation of thoughts and poems on society, for those whose only crime was non-conformity

This chapter is dedicated to those people who have struggled to 'fit in' to a society that demands defining. It is for those who faced stigma or difficulty with misconceptions and societal expectations. These thoughts and poems are an expression of some of the issues faced by people in an unforgiving, complex world of billions of people - Where we are all different, yet are expected to act the same.

Let Me Live by My Own Rules
Aren't we misunderstood by society?
Aren't we unheard by custodians of "right"?
Aren't we bogged down by senseless arguments?
Aren't we silenced when questioned why they are "right"?
It DOESN'T make SENSE?

51

Currency

This empty wallet speaks volumes
Unspoken words of unfulfilled dreams
Broken ties and unfathomable crevices
Of regret and desperation, tied as a noose

A coin of gold is what's aspired
A piece of cloth is what's desired
A handful of food is what's required
To live, hope needs to transpire

Confused and contemplating all this.....

Is it so hard to have courage
To stand by the son of a soldier who died

Is it so hard to have character
To call out the men who leave women brutalised

Is it so hard to be fair
To support a father who lost custody of his child

It is so hard to be human
To have compassion, let go of ego and pride

53

Life is an Aquarium

Life is an aquarium
Fake flora on the floor
Fake people seems the support
Fake colour of dreams

Memory of a goldfish
People's crimes against your mind
Clean walls that keep you "safe"
Keeping away from "scary" ocean

Is the glass keeping the fish in....or the people out?

54

Modern Slave

Tolling for hours to fill the plates
Drenched in silver bullets of the sweat
No dreams, no time to contemplate
Counting the days to give it all away

ꝒꝒꝒ

I am a Modern Slave
I am a Modern Slave
Lost and full of Regrets
I am just an Undergraduate

ꝒꝒꝒ

Drowning in despair and loans
Frowning at destiny's evil plan
Changing goals and life lanes
Recuperating from lost loves

ꝒꝒꝒ

Because I am just, just a Modern Slave
Lost and Full of Regrets
I am just, just a Modern Slave

Yeah it’s true, I am an Undergraduate
P.S.- I am a Post-Graduate

55
Confession

I preach you all every day
A delusional mind at bay
Nothing of value to say
Need your help and please pray

I am just a hypocrite, I know
Full of insane ideas to spew
I might've left something due
It's good for you, I never flew

It's time to stop this disgust
To let the mind to adjust
One day I will be my best
Will pass the society's test

56

High

A shot in vein, eyes dilated
Vivid dreams, I'm elated
It's a vice, you can't feel related
Stay away from getting devastated

Drugs work on scarred souls
It's the only thing to make them whole
A lie that they have been told
By movies, rap and rock and roll

57

Transient

Walk with me, see the stairs
People go up and down, no one stays
Such is life, nobody cares
You live or die, world spins everyday

You think you are centre of universe
This is a delusion, completely perverse
Listen carefully, allow it to transverse
Through your mind and soul, become diverse

58

Attention

Craving for attention on your post
You make faces and curl lips to pout
More likes are drugs that your snort
You lost yourself just to look hot

Get off the Instagram, it's damning
Your psyche is tainted, soul is drowning
These people seeing your stories streaming
Detest you as much as they can be

59

Expectation

It's suffocating, living in expectations
It's killing, all the dreams exploration
I have lived with a burden of people's interpretation
Of my abilities and my existence is just automation

Here we go again, with same sacrifices
Stomping on wishes because of other's whims
It will never end until I turn into recluse
Stay alone forever in my fortress of solitude

60
Exhaustion

I am a human, but living in a delusion
Fighting for ink on paper, a banker's creation
I see too far, but don't have a vision
I work with logic, no room for an emotion

Clock's pendulum reflects this life's suspension
No matter how much I swing, it's same oscillation
I observed from afar, looked at its position
Enclosed in glass, no one sees my exhaustion

61 Plastic Heart

I can't give my love anymore
To a person with a Plastic Heart
You only cared about appearances
Didn't care about my empty cart

I can't stand this whining
When I try to make ends meet
I paid for all your expenses
And you smile at bank teller who greets

I sketched but couldn't draw a line
I skated but couldn't escape the blame
I cooked but couldn't feed their ego
I danced even on their tune to survive

I wrote equations, couldn't solve my life
I wrote stories and poems, explain my mind
Now I have managed to escape the "template"
I want to be remembered as a Kind Man, only title that I aspired

63

Duality & Reality

She was my "Light" of my life
Light has dual character
A "particle" kept pounding me
A "wave" thrown me in despair

ᑭᑭᑭ

Who said Lighthouse saves lives?
Many ships wrecked by them
They give hope of solid ground
Never tell the rocky shore around

ᑭᑭᑭ

So why you are looking for light?
When men never respected it
They may guide you to a liquid path, and to ocean of despair

ᑭᑭᑭ

Sometimes destiny is revealed
At the end of despair
You can always walk alone, people will repair

ღღღ

You walked a thousand miles
I was inside my own trap
You changed so many minds
In course, mine got repaired

Final Words

"The Bartending Poet"

T his tale started long ago
H earing voices of a silent world
E xcited to know their dreams

♡♡♡

B elieving every word they said
A fter some time I realized
R eality isn't what's expressed
T here is an unsaid pain
E very sentence seems in vain
N obody cared to understand
D ismay of their friends
I nterrupted with the chaos
N ot finding order and sense
G iven this life as a challenge

♡♡♡

P eople who inspired me, I couldn't name
O ur conversations I cherish the most
E veryone told their emotion, a verbal game
T his book I wrote, is to honor people I serve.

9 798886 670721

Printed by Libri Plureos GmbH in Hamburg, Germany